Headhunter Poems

Ken Greenley

Illustrated by Angela Mark
Photography by Chuck Svoboda

Published by Improbable Productions

Denver, Colorado

ISBN: 0-9632326-2-2

This book is dedicated with love to my wife, Vicki,
also my teachers, Steve Michaud and Marc Crawford.

ACKNOWLEDGMENTS

Poems from this book have appeared in *Big Hammer* and the anthology *Cost of Freedom*, also online at *Outlaw Poetry* and *Short Story-UK*. I'd also like to thank Dave Roskos, John Richey, Matt Borkowski, Mike Romoth, Chuck Svoboda, Lenny Chernila, Barbara Test, Julie Cummings and Neil Kelly for encouraging me with my work and being the people they are. I'd also like to thank the old Court Tavern in New Brunswick, New Jersey and Ziggie's Saloon and the Mercury Café in Denver, Colorado for being the type of places they are.

CONTENTS

Headhunter Poems

Outside the Box

Think outside the box

the box is a coffin

And watch out for people

who smile too much

Those are fangs

Don't get in the hole

that's a grave

Beware enticing, fenced-in lawns

those are graveyards

Keep above the ground

Preferably moving

That's your job

That's your job!

Think outside the box

the box is a coffin

Don't get in the hole

and watch out for those big, enticing lawns

Because

Because there is death

I try to keep makin it

Because it is a dark age

I try to find the light

Because there is no hope

I'm optimistic

Because we are doomed

I feel invincible

Because days are numbered

I make every minute count

Can't threaten a guy who's already condemned

I use the power

of the death, darkness, doom and despair

against itself

in a metaphysical jujitsu

thus harnessed

it powers my machine

better get outta the way

don't you be wringin your hands at me

cause there's a big shit stomper chomper

money-makin machine

out there tearin apart the world

and you don't know what to do about it

Take away your black pom-poms,

oh cheerleaders of death!

I go to join the Animals

who always

creep

      crawl

                    scamper

   and fly

forward   full speed

Because

they don't know any better

Dead Cans o' Dad Beer

Walkin through the woods

found a crumpled box

a scattered pile o' cans

Dead cans o' Dad beer sittin in the woods,

Dead cans o' Dad beer drunk by teenage hoods,

Dead cans o' Dad beer couldn'ta tasted good.

Looks like

some little punk kids

stole some Dad beer

Reingold or Black label,

Schaefer or Pabst

some shit like that

swiped it out the garage

or down the basement

or wherever fine Dad beer is kept

Looks like

these little derelicts

went out and got

a coupla their cruddy little friends

then they took that bee-ah

and went out in the woods

to do some drinkin in the gully.

Dead cans o' Dad beer

attestin to the fact

Dead cans o' Dad beer

Young minds are out of whack

Dead cans o' Dad beer sittin in a circle

Little teenyboppers goin' all beserko

Dead cans o' Dad beer sittin in the woods,

Dead cans o' Dad beer drunk by teenage hoods,

Dead cans o' Dad beer couldn'ta tasted good.

Magnetic Colfax

Whenever I'm downtown

I feel an irresistible force

pulling me toward Colfax Avenue

like metal filings to a magnet

Magnetic Colfax

body and soul inexorably drawn

the mind just goes along for the ride

as usual

I plunge into Colfax the river

Tumbling out of the mountains and rolling east

its human salmon jump obstacles

on their way upstream

to spawn something

There I go into the shadow side of the street

with all the walkin the talkin

the drivin the beepin

the whisper the scuttlebutt the propositions

the rebukes

with the strutters and the smutters

and the hookers and the hawkers

and the dopers and the drunks

and the roughs and the toughs and the scruffs

here the smiles are more real

and missin a few teeth

join us at the Congress Lounge

as we break into a joint session

see weird shops with even weirder owners

it's all for sale on Colfax

hot and nasty

even the old men walk tough

right wing and left wing rubbing elbows

and sometimes the fur does fly

but a guy from a station there

loaned me a gas can once, no deposit

"Just bring it back," he growled

Highly magnetic Colfax

your broken down

roach-infested rooming houses

cheap motels and whorehouses

might indeed the eye offend

might cast a pall on the soul

but it also brings the feeling of something else

something called Truth

Colfax don't lie

like a lot of institutions and people today

Colfax

sticks its scarred, pockmarked face

right into yours and growls

"Yeah man, I'm Colfax!"

The Truth lives on Colfax

shouts itself

sings a siren song

body and soul inexorably drawn

like metal filings to a magnet

magnetic Colfax

I know I'll be pulled back soon.

Just Look at that Place

Tall weeds greet you

As you walk up the cracked sidewalk

The tall, unmowed grass

like the uncombed hair on an unkempt head

the front gate is missing a few slats

like a smile with broken teeth

the roof sags

It's missing shingles

the gutters hang low in bent bows

shutters hang off the windows

like puffy bags under a set of tired eyes

See how its weeds creep

See how its vines crawl

Dead trees drop dead leaves

Massive untrimmed shrubs

Seem to prop up its sides

the mailbox hangs crooked

under a faded, unidentifiable address number

Half the time the door is open

Come on in, if you dare....

The only house like this left

on an upwardly mobile block

Where most of the old houses

have been scraped off with bulldozers

and replaced with McMansions

The last of its kind

Like a lone buffalo in the neighborhood

and the neighbors know it

See how the sneers just drip off their faces

Disapproving looks

slide down plastic surgery noses

And bony, derisive fingers point

They shake their heads in disgust

Will you just look at that place?

The Bees Don't Want That Monsanto Food

Now the bees are disappearing

all over the world

There are those who say

that the reason is

They don't like those genetically modified crops

brought to us by Monsanto

So now these industrious creatures

that we rely on for cross-pollination

are leaving

Turning their nose up at that Monsanto food

Buzzing away from our bad diner

Crummy cuisine

Lousy service too

the humans don't respect

the customers no more

So they're blowin this tomato stand

Turnin their nose up at that Monsanto food

Gathering up into a crazy cartoon-like

angry black bee cloud

and droning away

into the blue crack of twilight

Never again to spread the pollen,

Never again to share the nectar.

Never again to spread the pollen,

Never again to share the nectar.

Gasoholic

Gasoline-addicted americans

Roar down the highway again

In their SUVs

Hummers

And Super-Sized Pickup Trucks

With names like

Sierra

Ponderosa

Ridgeline

and Sequoia

All-natural names

for very unnatural vehicles

That drink a lot

Gasoholic americans lean heavily

On brittle fossil fuel crutches

Hordes of them

Buzz like angry bees

toward an asphalt-cracked horizon

Gas pedals stomped

by millions of feet

Attached to brains

that somehow never make the connection

Between oversized vehicles

Rampant fuel consumption

and the irresistible urge

of their petro-dollar government

to invade weaker oil-producing countries

No sir

It's just drive, Drive, DRIVE

There's a shining star out there

on the horizon

for each of us

the constant promise of more, More, MORE

so off we go;

Reaching

Grabbing

Clutching,

Clinging

Devouring anything in our path

Like termites

Very little human about us now;

Cellphone, earplug, gadget things mostly

Just a mouth

Connected to an asshole

Nothing in between

Ram jet engines of consumption

Product is sucked in one end

Waste spews out the other,

who cares.

Creed

Let's all get in the holiday spirit

                      for the war

Let's all go shopping

            to protect our freedom

Let's all drive SUVs

            to show our love of nature

Let's all play with big toys

          while the rest of the world starves

Let's all be little emperors

                to exhibit our humility

Let's all be cold ruthless lying thieves

              and pretend

we're warm caring human beings

Let's all kick the door in

               to keep out the devil

Let's invade other countries

              to spread democracy

Let's bomb civilians

        and say we're their saviors

Let's rape and torture

        to uphold human rights

Let's all have a blood drive

        So we can spill more blood

Let's all dig mass graves

        for the foundation of new societies

Let's all scream

        That it's soaring when it's sinking

Hey you

        We said let's *all* do this

We don't see you participating

        What the hell's the matter with you?

Somebody call Security.

Vortex

At first

I hardly noticed it

This little black blob

lurking over the mountains to the west

But then as I looked out the window

It got bigger and bigger

Stronger and stronger

A churning mass of black clouds

Like boiling surf overhead

rushing our way fast

A disturbed, schizophrenic sky

changing from one color to another

Black, then yellow, then green, then blue,

then back through the whole range again

A weird array of colors

painted on the sky's palette

Mountain-high billows of cloud

seemed to stretch up into the sky's infinity

With lightning flickering behind them

Making them glow from inside

Thunder seemed to crack the sky in half

Sounding like a huge explosion

I walked out front to see what happened

And saw the whole neighborhood outside

Everybody from every house it seemed

Fingers pointing up at the sky

Everyone looking up

Hair blown straight back by the wind

Garbage and newspapers

whipping through the street

As the wind howled through the neighborhood

And that dark, troubled mass of clouds

blew right over us

filling the whole sky like black ink

spilled and spreading

Then the whole neighborhood gasped

As a gigantic cumulus charged across the sky

A weird, light color

against the rest of the darkness

Rushed in just to the north of us

A long crazy corkscrew shaped cloud

Shot right out its side

lashed out like the tentacle of a monster octopus

twirling crazily

reaching, grasping,

finally grabbing a foothold on the ground

I remember thinking

that's not how I thought it would look

As a large, expanding funnel cloud

Started dancing along the ground in the distance

the far distance, luckily for us

The siren on the roof of the nearby school

shrieked its warning

But we ignored it

Just standing there transfixed

Feet glued to the spot

Braced against the howling wind

Listening to its freight train roar

Standing there

with our hands covering our ears

to shut out the sound

of the warning

Until it just veered off to the northeast

and headed out toward open prairie

Tore up some turf

Ripped down some cottonwoods

and roared out toward open space

thank God

April

Now the long days;
rays of late sun
stretch the bare-tree shadows
Nascent warmth
reaches cold bulbs in ground
New shoots rise
through rain-soaked earth
Awakening

April
month of promise
but month of disappointment
Month to look forward
yet month to look back
Cool days, reminder of winter
warm, a summer foretaste.
Eight o'clock light
yet still cold

some trees naked,

others bold

Warm sun

But cool shade

soil turned with new spade.

Dark purple bellies

of Good Friday clouds,

tree silhouettes are crosses.

Birds herald

the coming of warm glow;

in hidden whistling song.

April, reverse October

Our part of the world tilting

closer to the Sun.

April, the promise of buds

olive shades

against grey skies threatening rain.

April, new green

lights up the grass

foretelling sprinkler rainbows.

April

Sunburst potpourri

Flecks of color

fill bare-branch frames

slowly spreading

light brushstrokes

o'er the landscape

the canvas of Spring.

Aboard Canoe

Tubular body

Plying through waters still

reflecting forest green

Boat's sharp silver bow

points like arrow to the sun

Twinkling

Our own private star

Come with us

As we paddle ashore

and feel the cool of green

seeking the shadow

between three trees

soft black space

surrounded by leaf jade

feel the peace and safety

there

Old Sneakers

My two old pals

the end of a long march has come

you used to be dazzling

you used to be stars

All-Stars in fact

Your new suction cup treads

smelling of vulcanized rubber

held fast to the surface of the court

made sharp cuts on tile and wood

stopped on dimes with loud squeaks

Now treadless you lay limp on the floor

ripped-up, ragged, dirty and downtrodden

riddled with holes like a rubbed-out gangster

but I'm the baby face

when I think of the glorious walks

we've been on together

climbing steep mesa inclines

weaving through canyons

stalking deep dark woods

collecting sand on long beach walks

soaked by ocean, lake and mountain stream

old sneakers together we jumped for rebounds

ran from cops and kicked cans

did drunken stumbles

suffered through long resigned walks stranded

one foot in front of the other you kept me going

oh how I'll miss our pedestrian peregrinations!

oh canvas carcasses

the box i bought the new ones in

serves as your coffin

bound for a landfill sarcophagus

it's been a long stomp

but it's the end of the stroll

Farewell canvas comrades!

My forward footsteps will look back

and remember you!

For George Reeves

George—George

Superman

the first one—the first time

that time of greased-back hair and midi-skirts

and huge cars with long rounded lobes.

Starched white hero

flying through the clear sky of a simpler time

the good guys

clean-cut, polite, wearing suits & ties,

the bad guys

slapstick goons with names like Mugsy or Lefty

"Hey Mugsy,

put de money in da bag and tie dem up"

But then you

would come busting through the wall

to save the day

I remember the pride swell I rode

knowing that good would always triumph

over evil

I was a lot younger then

I used to yell at you to watch out

As the bad guys tried to shoot you

Their exaggerated waving of their guns

as they fired

I can still see your no-nonsense expression

as the blazing bullets bounced off your chest

I remember your merciful reaction,

just knocking the bad guys' heads together

and leaving them for the police to round up

a true guardian of justice

even though your friend Inspector Henderson

used to beat confessions outta people

"Still won't talk, eh?" rolling up his sleeves

but he was beatin up a bad guy

and it was back then, so it was ok

ah, but even a Superman can't stop the clock

we grew tired of the squeaky clean

and started digging down-to-earth Anti-Heroes

and left you standing there

a Superman w/o a job

things weren't so simple anymore;

you tried on other roles

but they said no, you're Superman

no one will believe you as anyone else

Stuck as Superman

as we styled into rainbow clouds

and wailing guitars

and you sat like a rusting Studebaker

in a junkyard

and despaired and ran out of $

and then you—Superman

took your last flight

when we were kids in New York

and watched you on Channel 11

there was a running argument—

did you shoot yourself

Or did you jump off a building

thinking you could fly

Dirty Harry Poem

You shouldn't write a poem for Dirty Harry

But I'm gonna anyway

Got a problem with that?

Do ya feel lucky, punk?

Well ya should

Because It's always up to Harry

to walk in and fix it

when we reach the end of the game

of hot potato

we play with social problems

Dirty Harry

imaginary social janitor we've conjured up

Custodial caped crusader

DIrty detergent

Created and written by committee

various attributes

slapped on by various directors

patchwork quilt of justice

Dirty Harry

Justice robot we send out

as finally we wash our hands of it

Dirty Harry marching in

stiff-lipped and steely-eyed

administering justice unflinching

executing the sentence

Harry always absolutely sure

absolved of all our reasonable doubts

A few people might get killed

but Harry doesn't mind if we thank him later,

When we've seen the light

It's always Harry where the buck stops

Always Harry left to clean things up

And us running when we see the broom,

It's always Harry pursuing justice

and us walking the other way

It's always Harry

who walks through the minefield

while we go have a beer

It's always Harry who faces the gore we made

with a steady even gaze

It's always Harry

And a blank space where we should be

It's always Harry

Dirty Harry kicking down the door

rushing in to save the day

So we don't have to.

All Hail Cartoons

All hail cartoons

the lower consciousness

no high-minded righteousness here

no attempts to make it 'better'

just break a bat over their head

blow em up with a cannon

or the old standby—push em off a cliff

they just don't give a shit

in cartoons the lower consciousness

the tough as nails protagonists

keep on rollin

comin right back for more

charred, tattered

patched together with band-aids

sometimes crutchin it in a body cast

I like the ones that end in hell

cartoon hell

the protagonist chased out to the horizon

by a seething enemy

holding an ax or shotgun

sometimes driving a tank or a steamroller

anything possible in cartoonland

All hail cartoons, the lower consciousness

Pay homage to their ancient wisdom

their stone-simple philosophies

down to earth dogmas a person can grasp

Us vs. Them

don't be a dinner

survive the cartoon

All hail cartoons, the lower consciousness!

Life

Everybody looks up

as I walk down the hall

of the Senior Care Facility

The way my boot heels

clomp on the tile floor

gets their attention

in this place

where wheelchair-bound bodies

line the walls

and chins hang down on chests

Now most of the heads have bobbed up

Eyes wide open, hopeful

that someone will take them

Away from this place

But I can't do that

I have someone here myself

my wife's mother

struck down by a stroke

Not much time left

I have to stay here too at her bedside

My wife and I take turns

Deathwatch

We try not to see the fear in each other's faces

We don't know what to say to each other

Words can't convey it

It's too big and powerful

Smothering all

Only the sound of my boot heels

can defy it

Somehow the sound of them

clomping down the hall

speak an unspoken language

One that makes people's heads bob up

And eyes pop open hopeful

They know the sound

when they hear it;

Life.

Gone

When it comes to get ya

You're gonna try to run

but yer legs ain't gonna move

When it comes to get ya

You'll try to raise your arms to block it

But your arms ain't gonna raise

When it comes to get ya

You're gonna flip and flop

and try to fall out the bed

But you won't be able to move

No how

When it comes to get ya

You're gonna huff and puff

and try to catch yer breath

But they'll be no breath to catch

When it comes to get ya

You're gonna try

and try to stay

But you'll be gone, baby

Gone.

No More Two for One Days

Walking into the thrift store

Besieged by a crowd of old ladies

Seeing it's a two for one day

Ah yes, two for one days at the Thrift Store

I remember and smile, thinking how much

my wife's mother would have loved this

Two for one days, Ken

and a big grin

Then joining the other grey heads

bobbing up and down the aisles

Two for one days

and a mob at the door

Two for one days

and a hobbling rush down the aisles

Two for one days

and old ladies in their glory

Only now

Our old lady

She can't go

The entrance

looks all blurry

as I walk up

I turn away

Can't go in now;

Crying.

Your Ashes

I screwed up royally

When we went to scatter your ashes

My friend

I couldn't get it right

Couldn't get your ashes

into the wind the right way.....

Michael, Andrew and I

went up into the mountains to do it

Found a beautiful spot in the foothills

Walked till we found an appropriate cliff side

to scatter you from

It was a good spot with a great view

The first big peaks of the Rocky Mountains

seeming to reach out and touch us

A huge valley stretched out

between our rock perch and the mountains

On a clear day you can see infinity from here

Michael said

And we could have

Until huge clouds suddenly rolled in

And a raging storm began

Wind, a sudden coldness

Thunder, lightning, and sideways slashing rain

I remember chuckling (a little)

thinking how you would have said it was corny

When it finally passed

Becoming just the scattered patter of droplets

We got down to business

Andrew did it perfectly

Throwing your ashes up

and catching the wind

right as the gusts blew

Your ashes lifted up into the air

in little cloudlets

Just like they're supposed to

Just like in the movies

Maybe it was because he had a tiny teaspoon

I had a big tablespoon

and kept missing the gusts

So your ashes went into the air in clumps

Some of them coming back down

and hitting the ground with little puffs

or bouncing off the boulders behind us

or ricocheting off nearby trees

I tried to get it right, my friend

My heart was in the right place

Just wasn't scattering ashes real well that day

You would have laughed

I hope.

When I Go to Meet Them

After I die

And I go to meet them

Gods, light, a committee in the sky

or whatever they are

I hope when they see me coming

They're laughing

Because if not

They're going to very angry

They probably don't like the things I say to them

We argue

About various issues

like why did you take John Lennon at 40

and Nixon at 85?

And why do you allow

All this suffering

All these wars

and all this lying and stealing and killing

all over your world?

I get mad

Curse them sometimes

For the way they run the place

That's why I hope

after I die

When they see me coming

They'll be laughing

Because if not

They're going to be very angry.

#1 Responsibility

Back

in the first writer's workshop I was ever in

The man that ran it was very serious

He said writing was more than a course we took

More than something you learned.

It was a way of life

A different way of looking at things

He made everyone take their hat off

in respect to the craft of writing

whenever we met in the classroom

He respected it—and made us respect it, too

He reminded us how powerful words were

and made us mindful of their impact.

We appreciated it

wanted to hear more

We'd hang out together at a local bar

just off campus

We talked about the mysteries of writing

Late into the night

I remember one evening he said

The writer's #1 responsibility

was to remain alive.

Being twenty one,

I just snorted, well of course

and laughed like hell

Well, of course, he imitated my voice

in a whiney, sneering tone

it's always you young guys

that laugh real loud at that one.

His eyes got deadly serious

Under greying brows

taking slow, careful aim at me

Then he put his face really close to mine

and said

Maybe you'll live long enough

to see how true it is.

Don't Fall In

I remember well the times I was sent up

to work with the guys in Bulk Manufacturing

on the third floor of the cosmetics factory

where I worked the graveyard shift

as a young man

A substitute for guys who called in sick

Up I'd go in the elevator, to factory heaven

At least that's what my co-workers told me

They get to take it slow up there

an old codger

in the Creams and Lotions Department had said

You're gonna have an easy night

Grinning over my good luck the whole ride

The industrial elevator doors

opening with a loud creak

like the door of a monster movie horror house

Greeted by rooms as big as a football field

with incredibly tall ceilings

Like industrial gothic arches

Built to enclose

Huge vats the size of small houses

that rumbled and moaned

As they bubbled and boiled with the ingredients

of the shampoo we manufactured

for suburban, upper middle-class women

Which made hair silky and smooth,

just crying out to be touched.

My head tilted up in awe

at the massive silver cylindrical containers

clouds of steam whirling above

like mini manufactured meteorological systems

The overpowering sweet smell of shampoo

everywhere

I met the foreman

A big man with bulging fatigue-drained eyes

An industrial thousand-yard stare

He introduced me to The Guys

A longhaired unshaven bunch

All wearing bright green jumpsuits

And big black work boots

Young freaks, old codgers, middle-aged guys

from Eastern Europe and Central America

Come with me, the foreman said

leading me toward the simmering vats

beckoning me up the metal stairway

that looked like an erector set

His beard hanging over his uniform

Waving me up onto the metal catwalk

that surrounded the huge vat

a Captain Ahab of mass production

surrounded by whorls of steam

I looked down into the bubbling,

boiling ingredients in the vat

Huge beater blades reaching up from the bottom

circling like shark fins

roiling the gooey mixture

whipping the boiling froth

into a swirling, steaming whirlpool

A wall of sweet shampoo smell

nearly knocking me off the walk

We got one rule around here, kid

the foreman yelled over the racket

Don't fall in!

Night Shift Poem

Beams of the setting sun

awaken us into action

moonrise our call to arms

as shadows spread,

and darkness fills the window

We put on our uniforms

and our game faces

again

preparing for our nightlong struggles.

You, day people,

will never know our nocturnal existences,

our time-line diametrically opposed to yours;

as you settle into your couch

we contemplate our night-day ahead,

Waking thoughts creaking into motion

As your eyelids droop

we head to our stations,

Puddles of moonlight marking our way

as you drop off to sleep

we arrive,

Strolling in with a joke and a laugh

As your dreams begin

we pace empty skyscrapers, factory aisles

and wide warehouse floors

we do a hundred, a thousand jobs

you'll never see

a swarm of tasks taken for granted

As our solitudes and struggles,

arguments and actions continue

the outside world

plunges further into darkness

Ours is the chirp of cricket

the howl of dogs far away

the slither of slugs

and night-crawler worms

Bat radar and owl eye focus;

the beat of dark wing

and cloud drifting past full moon

the fog

the mist

and the smell of wet leaf,

also the tugboat's hoot

the train whistle,

and faraway factory pulse;

We're the hands on a clock

that won't move forward

Our night shift passing glacier-slow.

Like an exhausted runner

struggling toward the finish line

We finally make it

all the way to the end.

Released

into daylight

and the trip home,

eyelids drooping

muscles tingling

with the sweet buzz of staying up all night

Under cover of darkness

we've performed our jobs

when you left in the evening

the work wasn't done

when you come back this morning it will be;

Our shift a magic wand we have waved.

Shuffling back home

we meet people going backwards

rushing *to* work

instead of coming back

Morning people

                        day dwellers

                                           aliens

they head back to their stations

and we head back to our lairs;

two different breeds

crisscrossing

like nightshade

to a morning glory

or a stealthy barn owl

to dawn's busy chirpers

Clandestine workforce

hidden army

slowly marching home,

Elves

hiding just behind the veil,

the hem of night's cloak.

Cloud Watcher

Watching clouds

here in the foothills

of the Rocky Mountains

Just outside

a city that stands one mile

above sea level

Easy for the mind to take flight with the billows

Wouldn't think one mile closer to the sky

could make much difference

But it does

Leaning back

against a big boulder or tree trunk

One leg crossed over the other

Face pointed skyward

Eyes drift with clouds

Skyscape unfolds before viewer.....

High cirrus curl like brushstrokes

against an endless expanse of blue

Huge cumulo-nimbus

duel with dazzling sunbeams

Gigantic billows turn purple, then pink,

then flaming orange,

in the light of sunset's glory.

Clouds ten times higher than the mountains

press down on the tops

of the mountains themselves

above straight-arrow pines

Sky mural

Framed by green

Constantly changing

Ever-perfect

Watching it all, grinning

Soul speaks sky language,

saying thank you, thank you

to Whoever

or Whatever

made all this

I bow my head.

This is how I pray;

my pew, a fallen tree

my church, the forest.

Really Big Steps

I can't fly in my dreams

But I can take really big steps

I mean huge

Like a whole football field

Long soaring strides

Carry me when I sleep

I can't fly in my dreams

But I can take really big steps

I scissor-kick over high razor-wire fences

And glide above houses

I grab the top branches of trees

And swing sideways around them

like a horizontal pole-vaulter

Propelling myself high into the sky

I drift along, taking in birds-eye views

Of fields, forests, and faraway mountains

Of houses, roads and shopping centers,

A floating view of the fleeting grids of man.

I can't fly in my dreams

But I can take really big steps

I mean huge

The only problem is,

I have to come back down.

Old Man on Porch

At a house

Standing on the side of the road

that approaches my house

From the west

There's an old man

Who sits on the porch

I see him often

He looks real content

Relaxed, looking out

at the front faces

of the Rockies

as they curve off to the south

toward Pike's Peak

Many's the time I've seen him

As I return home from trips

to the foothills or mountains

At various times of day

Some mornings

he's in the shadow of leaves

shaded a soft green

In late afternoon

the sunshine

gives him a gilded edge.

In the evening brilliant beams

of the sunset shine upon him

lighting him with an orange glow

Just after sunset

he is enshrouded

by the soft blue light of dusk.

And somehow

Just seeing him

sitting there

looking out at his view

when I return home

is very reassuring to me.

Ray

Even as I traveled lost

down dark corridors alone

there was always a ray

A glimmer of light shining in

from somewhere

just a spot, gleam, or trickle

that found

and helped me

to stumble along

Even as I staggered

down murky twisting stairwells

Drunk out of my mind

looking at everything and everyone

cross-eyed and suspicious

Even as I wallowed

in tar pits of bad habit

My mind fogged by clouds

Even as I stormed

through red clouds of anger

my heart boiling with rage

Even as I punched and kicked

and slammed and broke my way

through life

Even as I lurched

through barren minefields of thought

not knowing who was my enemy

or who was my friend

Even as I dwelt in dark caverns

Even as I slunk through sewers

Even as I spun in deep whirlpools

Even as I slashed with shattered mirrors

There was still a ray

that shone in from somewhere

A skinny little beam

Tiny flecks of light on the wall

that somehow

Snatched me

from destruction.

City Playground

Life can be tough

on a small boy on a city playground

Nothing but steel and concrete

stretching for miles in every direction

Young eyes greedily grab

for space green freedom

I remember

How it was all left up to my soul's eye

How it transformed high brick walls

Into ponderous canyons

where Indians and outlaws

roamed wild

Holes in chain link fence

became portholes to other times

The playground blacktop

a night-time ocean

The basketball backboards hulking icebergs

And straight up

that small square of sky

enclosed by buildings

Seemed bluer

Reached higher

The clouds more free and drifting

Each one scarce

Precious

Don't Worry About Robert

Several years ago,

On yet another temp job

Everybody talked bad

about this guy named Robert

No Bob or Bobby, Robby or Rob

the ladies wanted to keep it strictly formal

with this guy

They said he didn't do his job

and made a lot of mistakes

dumped his work on others,

Just didn't care.

Lazy, stupid, shiftless Robert

also dirty and smelly Robert,

the women who sat near him

said he never took a bath.

Lazy, stupid, dirty, shiftless, stinkin-ass Robert

who openly fell asleep at his desk

with his head on folded arms,

Robert who could never do anything right,

the cause of everything bad at the office.

Robert would never amount to anything

Never hold down a job,

End up chronically unemployed

Go broke

Starve—die.

Well, I saw him just last week

Running to catch a bus

Leaning forward, top-heavy

Looked like he gained a little weight,

Big sack lunch in his lazy hand.

He appeared to be

In excellent health.

Monday

He looked like Monday

with his head hangin down

and his eyes all puffy and round

with his double chin and no grin

He looked like Monday

with his ass draggin

and his belly saggin

and his face haggin.

He looked like Monday

with his huffin and puffin

and his feet shufflin

with his loosened tie

and his bloodshot eyes

He looked like Monday

with his messed up hair

and his bad air

with his legs a-trudgin

and him hardly budgin

with his tattered fedora

and his worn-out aura

He hit the wall

And that's all

He looked like Monday.

Spin

Standing in the laundromat

looking through the dryer's little window

watching the clothes spin

reminds me of how life can be

jobs fly off to the side

Relationships careen out of sight

vices and bad habits

drift in from the side

swirl into the center

get mixed in with the fabric

consciousness trapped in the middle

pirouetting round and round

no reference point

my eyes bulge

whirling with the laundry

unable to deny the staggering similarity

hang on, hang on

I grab hold of the washing machines

behind me

to brace myself

take deep breaths

try to regain equilibrium

I look up the aisle

and see the old guy with the broom

he just looks back at me

at first I'm embarrassed

but then I see the look

in the crinkled eyes

Understanding

He knows

he's seen some things spin

out of control too

I Never Should Have

Instituted drinking

in the small park

by the bus stop

It was a bad move

Ill-advised

I didn't think of the social ramifications

I had just missed the bus,

after buying a six-pack

at the nearby liquor store

Then I saw the park

Handy, in a good spot

blocks from the bus stop

So I sat myself down

and drank a coupla beers

While I waited for the next bus

A peaceful half-hour spent

in the small, quiet park

little more than a small patch of lawn

Enclosed by a thin circle of trees

with a few benches thrown in

Still, it was kinda nice

Just sitting there, sipping beer,

looking up at a few stars

that I could just make out

above the brightness of the city lights

Finally, when the bus was about to come,

I said goodbye to my little park

and left, taking the empties with me

I try to clean up the messes I make

the physical ones, anyway

Now ya should see the place

Ya can hardly walk through there

Causa all the bottles and cans

and broken glass

All this other goddamn garbage

Those guys that came after me

and my pioneering effort

What a buncha slobs

Low-lifes, got no class.

I tell ya

Ya just can't crack a beer anymore

without an army o' creeps

following after ya and destroyin the place

I never should have

Instituted drinking in the small park

Near the bus stop

It was a bad idea

Ill-advised.

Sacrifice

Look how far

The concept of sacrifice

has devolved

In our modern society.

Used to be

Sacrifice

was something that had to be done

to keep the sun coming up

the weather going right

the streams flowing

the crops growing

Sacrifice

Something you just didn't skip;

Ancient requirement.

At least a portion of crop

given up,

Many times animals

Sometimes even ourselves

Our own blood spilled

to appease the Gods of antiquity.

As time went by,

parts of it fell out of favor

First the human,

then the animal

New currencies used;

Coins tossed into a basket

alms for the poor given

The concept slowly dwindling

to a grudging hour

spent in a church pew on Sundaes;

A rushed grace

muttered over Thanksgiving dinner.

Nowadays sacrifice

A distant spot

Seen over our shoulder

Far back on the road.

One has to look far and wide

for any sign of it

In today's

Me-first

outta my way

Gimme that

thousand toy

24-7 Big Sale

Modern world.

Sacrifice hardly ever done,

almost extinct now;

We've sacrificed

Sacrifice.

Second Great Depression Poem

A depression that doesn't acknowledge itself

a depression that says it's not a depression

a depression that calls itself a recession

then calls itself great

a depression we were not prepared for

Yet somehow expected all along

A depression we bought on credit

A depression we chose not to see

as soon as we saw it

A depression where the truth is hard to find

like a modern Diogenes

wandering around with his lamp

looking for an honest man

a depression that contradicts itself

a depression where the restaurants are full

and sometimes the bars

A depression where the stores still bustle

and people still hustle

and you wonder how, with what money…

A depression with inflation

A depression where the price of food

Keeps going up and up and up

And other commodities are right behind

A depression where

any   thing   costs   more

A depression with TV

with vicarious affluence cabled into each house

hypnotizing the audience into believing

they're one of the upper class

movers and shakers themselves

Though many of them are financially sinking

House upside down, underwater

Out of work or underemployed

A depression where 50 million of us

are going without health insurance.

A depression of people not keeping up

lots of them

not keeping up and hiding it

You can see it in the faces, though

Written as clear as invisible ink

A depression with no one to say

there's nothing to fear but fear itself

with no FDR to help us this time;

a depression with plenty to fear

including fear itself

a depression where the social contract is broken,

where the rich don't want to give back

a depression where the rich get a *tax cut*

during all this

and we have to tighten our belts again

A depression with deep cuts to social programs

a depression that kicks the poor

and the sick and the weak

to the curb even more

a depression with stingy republicans

corporations with huge profit margins

and lots of police in riot gear

a depression with large numbers

of pissed off people

road rage and public confrontation

and plenty of guns floating around, too

and some of the people holding them

ready to go off any minute

a depression that isn't fuckin around

a depression with rumors of martial law

and hidden prison camps

a depression of looking at the future and wincing

a depression we doubt we'll survive

A depression where it's up to you

to keep your spirits up

and the spirits of those around you

a depression of keeping our eyes

toward the light

tough job in a depression

but a job that needs to be done

a depression that maybe does show

that spirit and other intangible qualities

may actually count for something tangible

It does seem

to keep people's heads above the water

Swimming forward when they might have sunk

Seems to do something else too

Seems to jar something back to life in us

Bringing back things long forgotten;

A depression that might force us

to work together once again

A depression that might drive us

back into the garden

A depression that might turn us

back into human beings.

Tough on the Heights

They thought they were tough on the heights

and they patted themselves on the back

all the way up the mountain

Lovers of themselves

on steep cross-cuts

discarded mirrors seen alongside the trail.

They thought they were tough on the heights

And they stood spread-eagled on rocky crags

Looking down on the world

Smug looks on all the faces.

They didn't notice those black wings

Circling behind them

Or those gathering grey cumulo-nimbus

Or the darkening sky

Nor the shadows that fell over them

They didn't notice a lot of things

until it was too late

They thought they were tough on the heights.

Then   Thunder   Lightning

Rain   Fog   Cold

Crosscut trails turned to mud

Rock footholds

Now slick rock ramps

Leading only one way

They thought they were tough on the heights

Didn't notice those black wings

Circling behind them

Talons in the belly

the probable outcome all along

And they slipped and they slid

and they clawed and they clung

but they tumbled down bouncing

like sacks of potatoes

They thought they were tough on the heights.

Stealth Bomber

I heard it before I saw it

A loud roaring

over the back yard

Like a scraping against the sky

I went around to the front of the house

looked up

and there it was

a Stealth bomber

Flying right over the house

on its way to thrill the crowd

at the football stadium

My house is right between

the air force base

and the stadium

So every once in a while

One of their toys

strays into my airspace

this time pretty unbelievable

A big triangle in the sky

Black, sleek

Thought I might be seeing a UFO

What with the hangover I had

It swooped down over the neighborhood

Like a hawk, a metallic bird of prey

Roared over the next block

Then rolled, and leveled off

Turning to a thin, scythe-like line

As it whooshed away

Making the same sky-cracking sound

as it left

I guess whoever put on this show

wanted me to say ooh and ah

At their friendly version

of shock and awe

But it didn't quite work out that way

Instead all I could think of

Was what it would be like

to get attacked by one of these things

Especially if you were an innocent civilian

Like in so many attacks we read about

Imagine that—

You're making mud bricks in Afghanistan

or maybe looking out at your fields,

figuring out a way to water them

Kids playing outside

Wife inside making dinner

Then here it comes

That scraping, roaring sound

First your eyes strain to see it

A thin, sickle-shaped line in the sky

Growing exponentially

And before you can say

What the hell is that

It's right on top of you

A terrifying black triangle

Swooping down like a falcon

Missiles and bombs rain down

on your family

Your house disappears

in an earth-shaking

roiling fireball

Whoops—just another mistake

a little more collateral damage

That's what I thought about

When the Stealth fighter-bomber

Flew over my house

No pride or patriotism

No Washingtonian hubris or arrogance

Instead I saw their fighter-bomber

through the eyes of 'the enemy'

People in mud brick houses

On a faraway continent

Killed by extra-judicial remote control

For practicing the wrong religion

in the wrong place

right in the way

of one of their oil pipelines.

Headhunter Poem

No—the authorities were wrong!

I didn't shrink your head

I only brought it down to actual size.

Aw right—I'll admit it

I shrunk your head

Right there in my fireplace

It crackled like a yam in tin foil

Me sitting there in a contemplative state

As I nursed a vodka and orange Ne-Hi

Thinking how your head was very swollen indeed

Chock full of media lies

and propaganda

There was no heart to your head

Plus it didn't work right

It couldn't think for itself

I shrunk your head

because you thought you were Einstein

when you were bush league

Because you thought you were hot tuna

and you were cold as a mackerel

I shrunk your head

because you looked and never saw

heard but never listened

groped but never felt

because you were an uncaring

Unthinking

Unfeeling

Unyielding

           Obstacle

Know what—I'm done thinking about it

why I shrunk your head

It makes me nervous, and agitated

Enough—just shut up

and sit there on the shelf!

Weapons

Watching people shop

in the local gun store

trying on various handguns for size

Can be a sobering experience

A lot of these people don't look very smart

to know that they will be armed soon

Is a frightening thought!

Of course I'm right there in the store with them

But I'm different

I don't have the same expression on my face

that they have

That looking for an answer look

all over so many of the faces

They think that gun

is going to do it for them

They never see

that the most potent weapons

the mind   empathy

Political awareness   social consciousness

have been defused

and de-activated long ago

By the biggest brainwashing machine

in the history of mankind

The whole world shown through

a single corporate-military glass

the world their way

Repeated over and over

on every media imaginable

Most of the facts bent, twisted and muddied

Until any awareness,

Consciousness or compassion

Is slowly shrunken and shriveled

Atrophied and decayed

Until the mind

The most potent weapon of all

Has been rendered nearly useless

Social consciousness on life support

political awareness in america

Reduced to a kind of living death

Like being trapped inside a body

you can't control

As it runs amok

and destroys everything in its path

Powerlessness the main vibe

No matter what they say

That's where the average citizen

stands in america today

Powerless and unrepresented

It explains the looks on the faces

of the people in the gun stores

it explains the nature

of hearts and minds

of guns and bullets

Of weapons.

Poems

On my desk are malformed, defective poems

Limping and stumbling along

Struggling to come to life

They might make it, they might not.

On my desk are dead poems

Or poems that will soon be dead.

Nothing can be done,

They will be left behind

as other poems march ahead

On my desk are poems

That show signs of life

that have potential

To at least form themselves into words

Maybe light a fire somewhere sometime.

On my desk are stronger poems

with sails full of wind

Ready to cross wide oceans

and reach uncharted lands

On my desk are marooned poems

Washed up on desert islands…

Waving their arms frantically

To passing vessels

On my desk are poems that

can't wait to take off like rockets

into the stratosphere

Just able to see the stars

On my desk are poems

invisible

dream-poems

Still half in the ether

On my desks are poems

that aren't even poems

Yet.

Prayer

A prayer to stop world cops

and douse the dreams of oil-crazed old men

A prayer against Empire;

for all imperial designs to fail

A prayer for a return to balance of power

and the establishment of equal exchange.

A prayer for an end to world corporate takeover

A prayer that the whole planet

doesn't go into full robber baron mode

A prayer to stop more bank blackmail bailouts

and countries held hostage by the IMF

A prayer for an end to the World Bank as King.

A prayer for an end to greed dressed as virtue

For an end to misers disguised as heroes,

a finish to those who would take it all.

A prayer for a return to real political dialogue

For an end to empty campaign rhetoric

and pep rally conventions

and fake populists

who report to corporate masters.

A prayer for an end to people going broke

because they got sick

A prayer for an end to huge medical bills

A prayer for an end to all medical bills,

A prayer for an end to health care for profit

Forever.

A prayer for an end to drone aircraft attacks

extra-judicial killings and torture

A prayer for re-observance

of the Geneva conventions

and for the UN to act as protector

of all nations

not just the rich Western ones

A prayer for the defeat

of phony peacekeeping forces

everywhere

And an end to invasion

and infrastructure destruction

Disguised as the spread of democracy

A prayer for an end to world cops

and security freaks

We can look after ourselves just fine, thank you

A prayer for the plans of all Empire builders

to go terribly wrong everywhere

to run awry and unravel completely worldwide

A prayer that the whole

Bossy   grabby

Bloody   deathy

Meat grinding machine

Chokes on a bolt

 and blows a gasket

A prayer for everybody to just

leave each other the hell alone for once

A prayer for peace and quiet,

even if it's just for fifteen minutes....